On The Waves of An Odyssey

J. Friedrich Allyn

Cover art is an altered image of a drawing by Japanese artist Mori Yuzan in his 3-volume work *Homanshu*. This work is in the public domain and considered free use.

Copyright © 2021 J. Friedrich Allyn

All Rights Reserved.
This book or any portion thereof may not be reproduced or reused in any manner whatsoever without the expressed written permission of the author except for the use of brief quotations for a book review.

Send all inquiries to: BlackCouchLounge@protonmail.com

First printing, 2021

ISBN-13: 978-1-7340542-2-4

For the unrepentant dissidents

Journey to The End of Adventure	11
Whip	13
Not About Sex	15
Amour Fati	17
To Sucker a Sucker	19
Solution Manifest	21
Hippie of The Highbrow Hunters	23
Premature Maturity	25
The Pickaxe Artist	27
Desperate Divination	29
The Air Above Hedon	31
Bumbling	33
Grower, Not A Shower	35
Negative Intuition	37
The Sacrifice of Sundown Souls	39
Shredding The Sacred	41
Shalom, Shalom	43
Progressive Pirates of Priapism	45
Vapor Trail	47
Seek Death	49
8th Grade Reading Level	51
Be Careful Young Men	53
Haughty on The Ready	55

57	Feelings Are Fake
59	Ode to Order
61	Sigillum Dei
63	Pride on My Side
65	Artificial Sugar
67	Acrobat of The Abyss
69	Innocent Talk
71	Self-Awarewolf
73	Delicious Delight
75	Obstinate Empathy
77	Life Without a Pimp
79	Chimerical Animus
81	Postponed Percival
83	Elder Berries of The Salted Earth
85	Ephemiracle
87	Median Patience
89	To Commune
91	Devour Maternal
93	Level Up
95	Macho Robusto
97	Fear Filled Fealty
99	Push Pull
101	Playbook

Note on Illustrations:

The drawings within this book are some of what I affectionately call my *creatures*. I have drawn them since my early teens by simply closing my eyes, making a mark or two on some paper, and adding in human features, giving them some form of life. Over time I developed a particular style, in part born out my lack of realistic drawing talent and skill, that made them even more creature-esque, with some falling more on the silly or whimsical side and others carrying a darker, more Rorschach test vibe.

I kept them mostly private, sometimes showing a close friend or lover, and I wasn't sure if my hiding them was insecurity related to creating such strange looking things or if there was something more personal, even more unconscious, than even I knew. I eventually came to realize that I was attempting to personify my emotions as separate from myself in an effort to understand and process them. Naturally, as I made this realization, I began to create them much more deliberately, and they even started to become more complex as a result.

I have also written poetry for about the same length of time, so when I decided to produce a book of poetry it felt right that I should also include my creatures, as they served the same function as poetry in many ways, just a bit differently.

My hope is that while reading this book the reader will have both sides of their mind stimulated at the same time, and it is formatted with this purpose in mind. Each drawing and its accompanying poem *do* correspond in terms of their premise, even if they don't correspond in terms of details.

Each drawing is an original creation of J. Friedrich Allyn, enhanced, illuminated, and brought to life by the wonderful work of artist John Denmat.
Instagram: @johndenmat & Email: Jdenmat@gmail.com

Journey to The End of Adventure

On the waves of an Odyssey,
I hitchhiked in time.
Book marking no insights,
At empty tables I dined.

The music of the past rings fresh in my ears,
With vibrations of desires made abundantly clear.
I made my own language for expression in secret.
But characters aren't clean, so I didn't quite get it.

Try as I might, I can't fix what fate broke.
There's no Zen to this manual,
Just piles of post-it notes.

Whip

I set to task a discipline,
With all my demons snickering.

I drove a nail and hung a whip,
And when they spoke, I cracked their lips.

My rules were neat and glistening,
They smirked but called it interesting.

Over time they did submit,
And to my will they did commit.

I set to task a discipline,
With my imps resolved to listening.

Not about sex

A tilt of the neck,
A shifting in vision,
A curl of the waist,
Invade the incision.

Affection withheld,
Lustfully compelled,
Take up defense,
Get high on the stench.

Sexual allure,
Yet violently pure,
Shallow scrapes to subside,
And pain you can't hide.

Skin on cold concrete,
Marking defeat,
Quick to your feet,
Completely discrete.

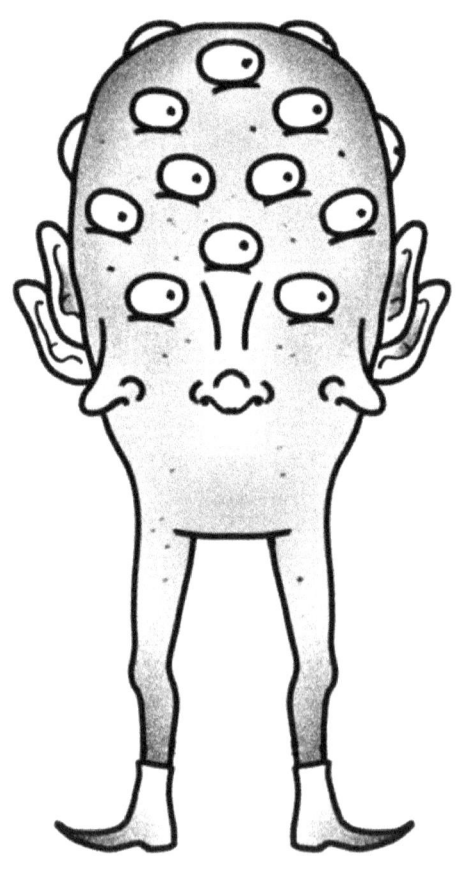

Amour Fati

A timeline of change,
A brief history of wisdom.
Teach me the pain,
Of condemned inner reign.

Observation is key,
To learn how to be,
Accidents are fake,
Trouble, for my sake.

I lie, wide awake.

To Sucker a Sucker

The clash of fallen stars,
Cut your feet and slowed your stride.

The chill of radiated rocks,
Caped the knees of my once coward pride.

I know your stance,
And you know mine,
I'm superior, To everything, You're inferior.

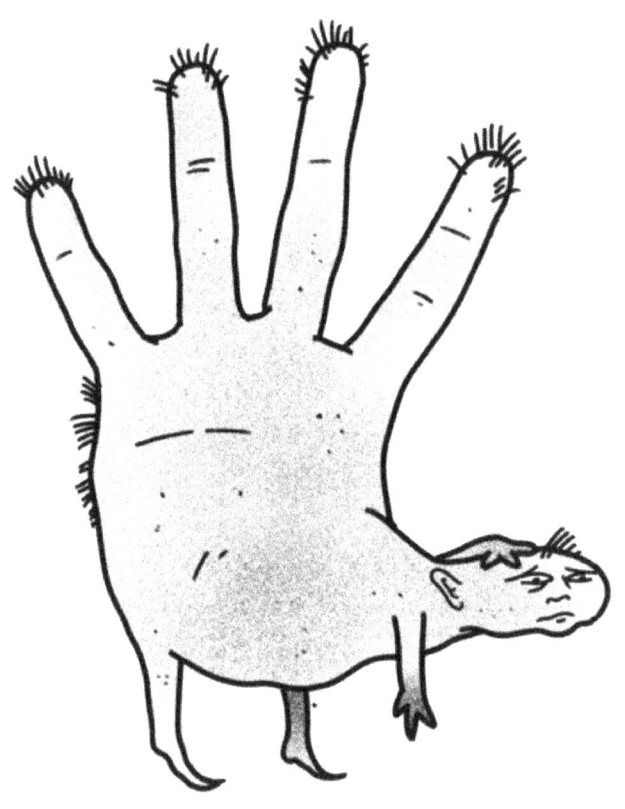

Solution Manifest

Infatuation maturation,
Manifestation saturation.

Congregation concentration,
Participation satiation.

Gentrification affectation,
Good ol fashion masturbation.

Hippie of the Highbrow Hunters

No destination, no end in sight,
Hurricane sailing, backward in fright,
We blister our hands, but the course doesn't right.

We skipped rites of passage,
A plus LARPing like a faux muddy savage.
And stalling our growth with crass phony badges.

We want to live large in sappy teen shows,
Sense weighted words with hints of pop flows,
And sell everything in weak trampled rows.

We look at the night to conjure sunsets,
Dance sexy and stupid to all the right sets,
With eyes burning bright from hedging our bets.

We take late-night walks conversing with trees,
Peer out of square windows to shy ready streets,
And infatuate felons on pale skinny sleeves.

We want all the feelings that keep gaming fate,
Look back and smile at marks on wood gates,
And hike hollow cities of loud ticker take.

We throwback our heads and pretend we hold class,
Leave tracks in the grass from slurred midnight mass,
And lament an embrace that ends way too fast.

We seek constant joy in the saddest factory,
Snare oak aged memories to year 33,
Pure, in a sense, immaturity.

Premature Maturity

Excitement breeds' speed,
And panic takes hold,
Static sans problem,
This is me being bold.

Collapse without words,
Humid filled throat,
Briar stuffed stomach,
Feeling comes remote.

Of Virgins pain we complain,
Hot peppers by the pound,
The priest prescribed bitters,
Yet we tenant farm sugar cane.

The Pickaxe Artist

Set your vacuum to blow,
Inhale deep on filth.

Move back, move forward.
Restless legs and a restless soul.

What are the eyes even for?
Look and see as the stomach turns.

Where is the living fire?
Syphon it in, production turned foul.

Stalemate after stale mate,
A dugout routine throwing dirt in the air.

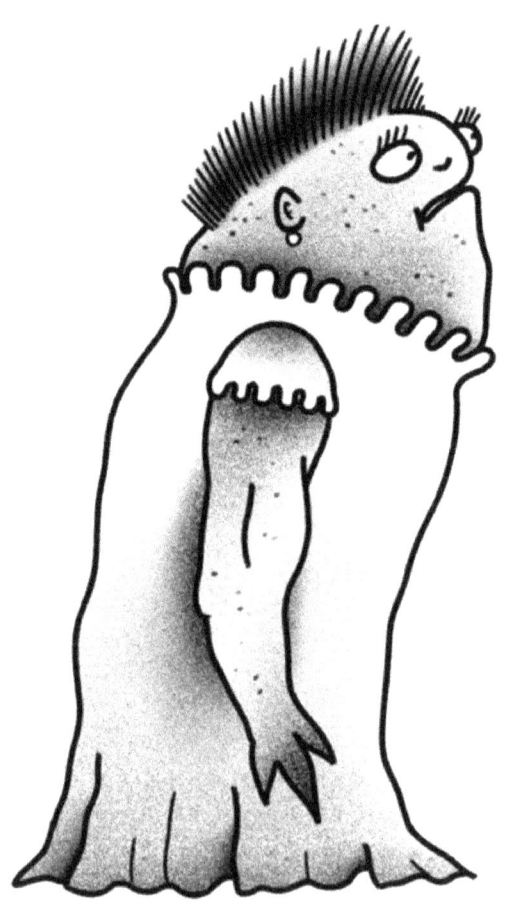

Desperate Divination

The cards predict pain,
The Stars suggest sorrow,
The moon set to wane,
No sun left to borrow.

The bones turn up empty,
The birds augur loss,
No coffers of plenty,
The numbers have a cost.

The clouds collect rain,
The trees wave till hollow,
The tea leaves they drain,
No nutrients to swallow.

Your job with no boss,
My wall with no sentry,
Out actions turned frost,
And hearts barred to entry.

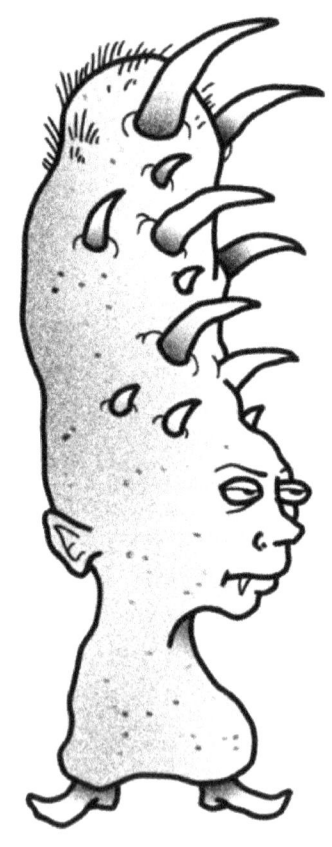

The Air Above Hedon

Here I plunge,
Into the wild,
Seeking affection,
Just like a child.

I wish I may, I wish I might,
Have the courage to treat her right.

Bed her fast or make it last,
There is no gray matter saved in the past.

I feel the ideal,
Will it be real?
I sense the expense,
My hands I must rinse.

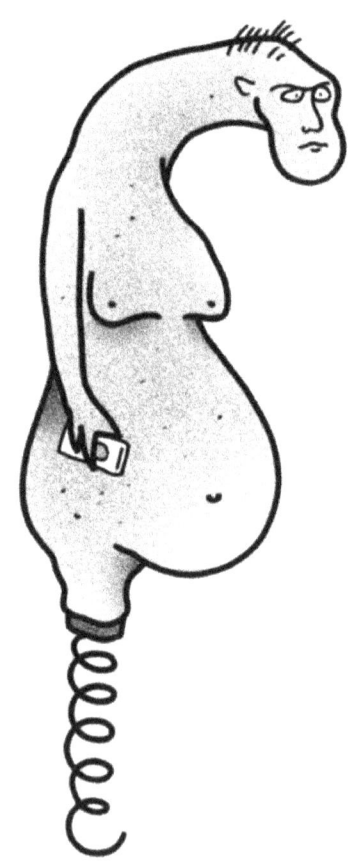

Bumbling

Grumble grumble mind frame fumble!
External conditions have ruffled positions,
Forcing my thoughts to break with tradition.

Humble humble ego in tumble!
Emotional periods projected in mass,
I've poisoned the air with unmanly sass.

Crumble crumble state in a jumble!
The full moon came and washed up a crab,
I may need a nap, just call me a cab.

Rumble rumble heart all a bumble!
A harness is needed to wrestle this spirit,
Victory is sure if only I will it.

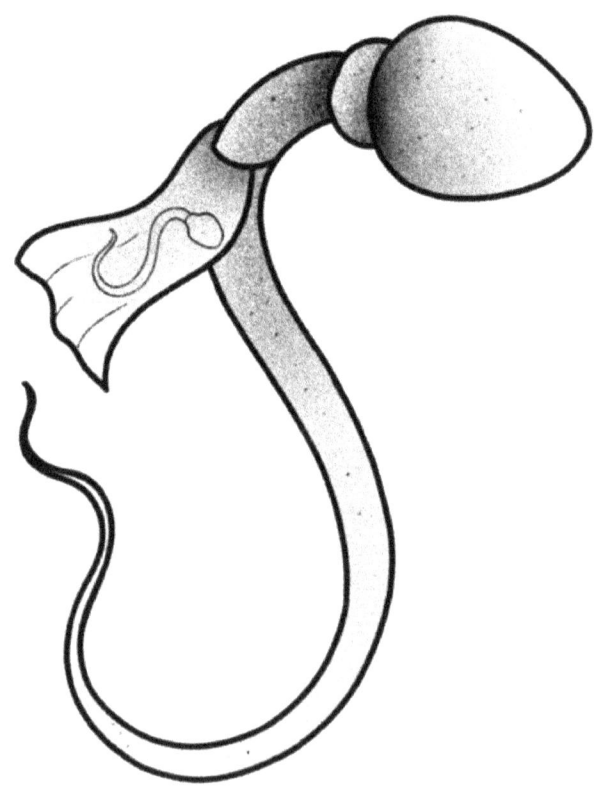

Grower, Not A Shower

Fleeting emotion
Full of commotion
Deep as an ocean
No need for lotion.

Quiet rejection
Social ejection
Negative erection
Still no direction.

Disposable dancer
Despicable manners
Bar fly scanner
Character scammer.

Childish affection
Idealized projection
Shadow injection
Realistic correction.

Selfish devotion
Falsified notion
Perpetual motion
Poisonous potion.

Negative Intuition

With confidence uprooted,
The long hours come looting.

Substantial slumber disturbed,
Potential moments lay curved.

Fumbling and faulting sprung from overdone halting,
Eyelids lay heavy and long sighs come wafting.

Breath in, Breath out, no reason to stress.
Just as I guessed, fully enmeshed.

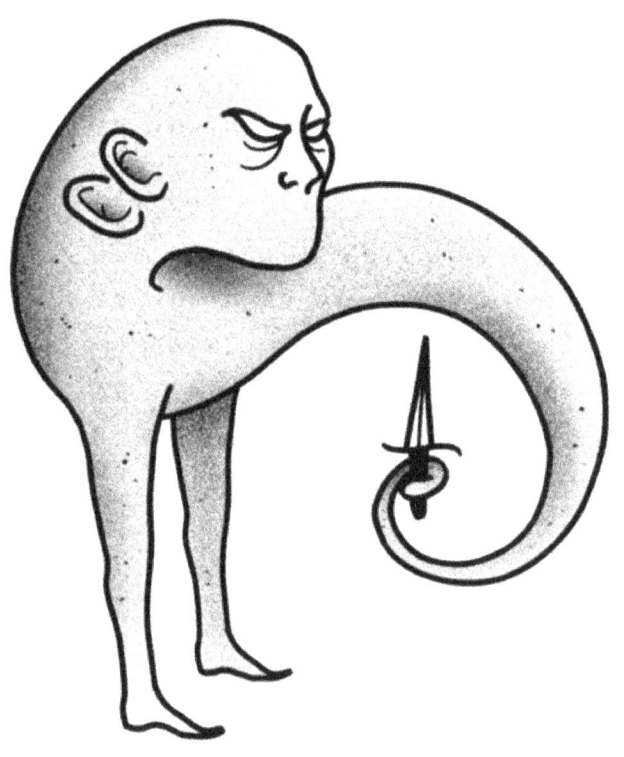

The Sacrifice of Sundown Souls

Shed all your armor, your keychain adventures,
Put down your sword and release all your censors.
It's time to be humble and observe all your senses,
Retard your communion with raised up defenses.

Pull off your boots and strip off your shirt,
Cut off your beard and dig deep in the dirt.
The movement of silence adds spice to the air,
As vibrations and visions intrude unaware.

Break all your fingers and gouge out your eyes.
Pull out your hair and shrink down to size.
The collective is here and happy you came,
Do you want to be new or stay just the same?

I hear the alarm; I see the late hour.
I wait for the fall; do I jump from the tower?
From this act I do cower, and shrink at the thought,
The event becomes sour, my limit is caught.

Shiva! Shiva! I call unto thee!
Dance out your fires and boil down the seas,
I can't see your eyes when they penetrate me.

Shiva! Shiva! I call desperately!
Lift up your scales and untangle the keys,
I want to be lost in the beauty of ease.

Shredding the Sacred

We dove to the bottom of what seemed so real,
Found all was delusion, a gypsy's appeal.

We dug up the stones and shifted the sand,
They all broke apart and out of our hands.

Found nothing was true, except we were skilled liars,
And here in this place we can't build a fire.

I stood up tall and made a command,
"We leave this place for the sunny dry land."

You didn't look up, you just kept digging,
Wearing a scowl with a tone unforgiving.

I came to my senses and pressed hard with my toes,
Pointed my feet and led with the nose.

I tried for your hand, but you wanted to stay,
Deep in the darkness of a feeling's melee.

I'm swimming for air and the sun to replace,
The darkness within and this poisonous embrace.

Because watching you drown, and turn into waste,
Is boring & lame, and absent of grace.

Shalom, Shalom

Shalom, Shalom, Give in to the dawn.
This fight is my plight I accept it all right.

How's that go down? Down like a whore!
I'm done with the act I don't want it no more.

Stare at the night. Jump in the fire.
This night is too bright, like an innocent liar.

What's that you say? Tell you the truth?
I see you in pain, but I stand here unmoved.

Shalom, Shalom, Return to the source.
See where it started and plot a new course.

Shalom, Shalom, Third time's a charm.
I tried to do right, didn't mean any harm.

Shalom, Shalom, Let's try it again.
Turn down the bed as midnight creeps in.

Shalom, That's it! I'll give you the scoop.
You can choke on yourself; I've set the mood.

You challenged my hand,
I've answered your call,
And here's the best part,
I'm not sorry at all.

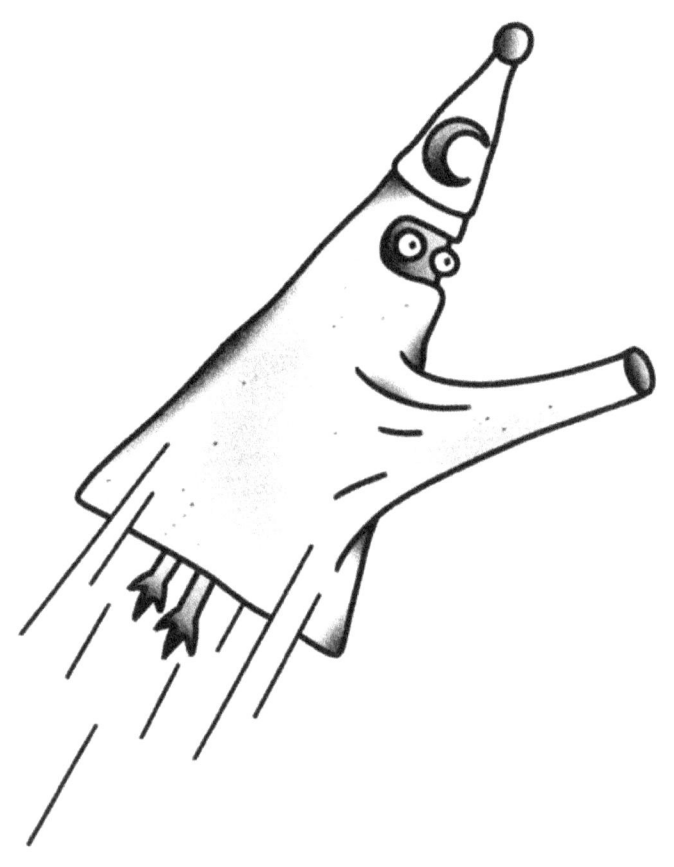

Progressive Pirates of Priapism

The razors edge was hot as hell,
On outdated trivia cards wishing us well,
Appetizing screams that kiss me deadly,
In the cake icing wisdom of a rotten fruit medley.

Rolling over six times in a cold sweaty bed,
We found a cure to make us as good as dead,
Stream it full force and choke on the cope,
Young tarts smile and swing our death rope.

Trip over cracked concrete that snaps bleeding silk,
My generation suckled on foreign mothers' milk.
We take up black sails and pack up the cats,
As the past is recorded in the tears of our car mats.

Vapor Trail

Reading the words and seeing the sights,
I have no defense and don't have the right.
Drama too much and you might get sick,
Adapt to abuse and get used to it.

Tension filled air and a question filled heart,
How to make sense, to tear it all apart.

Expressing expressions on sleeves over worn,
Generations of language over adorned.
Missing the message in gardens of feign,
Find a new tell and start over again.

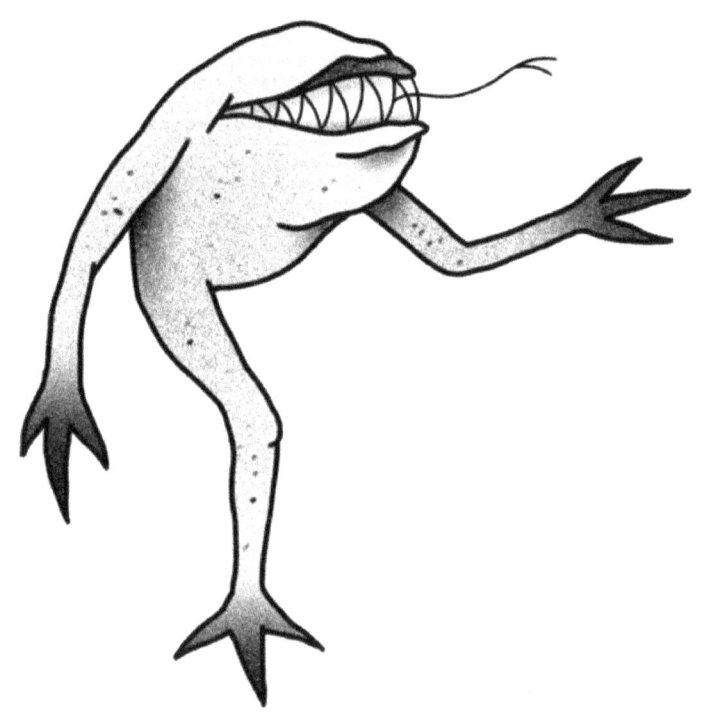

Seek Death

With airy vibrations and fogged condensations,
I deliver my message for no compensation.

I ask only this, you must know who you are,
Avoid all excess yet shoot under par.
In addition to this you will offer your life,
The payment is sealed with your sacrifice.

Pay not to me, for I am not He,
Death is the debtor, who else could it be?
Turn and face fate, but live a full life,
He's not what he seems, and his socks are pure white!

With eyes to see and ears to hear,
The truth will always be ready and near.

Seek death my friend, I promise you this,
Take his dark hand and learn how to live.
Do you seek glory and infinite bliss?
Well what kind of life do you have to give?

8th Grade Reading Level

Focus is nil,
Motivation is still,
Attention deficit of a stressed precedent.

Excuses galore,
Escapist whore,
Memory imprint is insignificant.

Repetitive drilling,
Ready and willing,
A triple extreme of forgotten dreams.

Be Careful Young Men

The power of woman is oft overlooked,
Her intuition not understood,
With this power you're hooked,
And made hers for good.

She molds you to man,
Her work is never done,
Her vision an ideal,
She only serves this one.

Regardless of image,
She fits you to frame,
Begs you conform,
Be the victor of her game.

The pull is instantaneous,
Especially when young,
The boys are unaware,
All they want is fun.

The strongest still fall prey,
When we least expect it,
Nothing much to say,
We all grow to accept it.

Choose carefully young men,
And know who to be,
Your woman makes it happen,
When you become daddy.

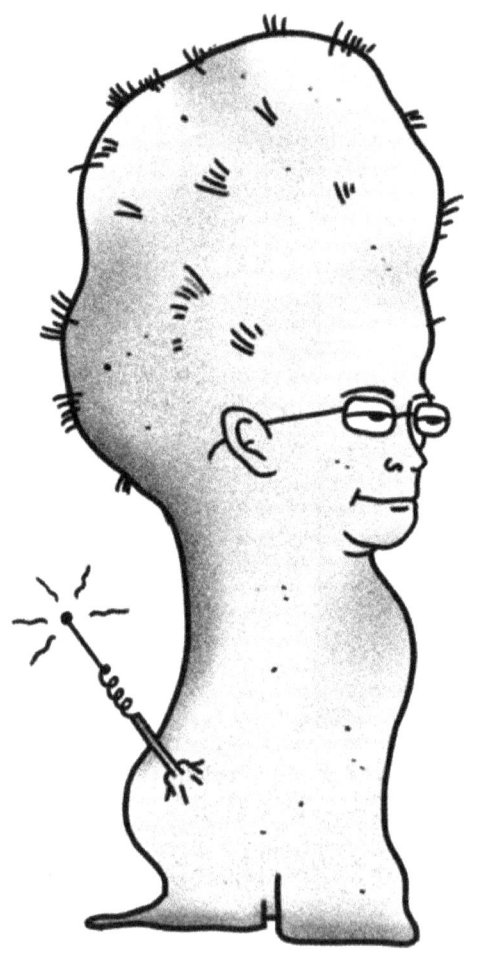

Haughty on The Ready

I sit here in one of my most arrogant moments.
Congratulating myself for moments not occurred,
Gloried potentials in the past, lazily inferred.

Overwhelming pride,
Confidence on my side,
The mind opened wide,
Spewing universal asides.

I can't go to work; I can't read a book.
I can't think of me with my ego in the way!

I don't hold it against me,
But I detect a faux pas.
Do others not agree?
They don't hold me in awe?

This must be a defect,
To realize imperfection with so must power to effect!

So, to all my friends and family,
Since you are here to serve me,
I have a task for you.

I should never have had to tell you,
To join me in this project.
Correct me, because I'm wrong.

I invite you to look at me, listen to me,
And most importantly,
Laugh with me, at me,
In spite of me.

Feelings Are Fake

The puddles are too deep,
The oceans are too mean,
The rivers won't keep,
And the lakes can't stay clean.

                                      The sea rises up,
                                      The rain seeks appeal,
                                      The ice is too corrupt,
                                      And the ponds will dirty deal.

The streams are far too sleazy,
The swamp is far too cool,
A bath is just plain lazy,
And the shower always pools.

                                      The drips slowly build,
                                      The dam will not hold,
                                      The flow goes to field,
                                      And tears just grow old.

But the puddles will deplete,
And the oceans will lose steam,
The rivers make great leaps,
And the lakes turn pristine.

                                      The sea will envelop,
                                      The rain emits a squeal,
                                      The ice will develop,
                                      And the ponds learn to heal.

The streams all turn easy,
The swamp proves a fool,
A bath cusses cozy,
And the shower drains full.

                                      Drips will congeal,
                                      A dam gathers mold,
                                      The flow grows a yield,

                  And tears prove us bold.

Ode to Order

You ordered this ode as a speech about love,
Like a fast-food consumer out on a date.
Love is a parasite that disorders all things,
Like a fart in a car, no one escapes.

Love has the power to change your whole life,
Like an unwanted pregnancy, discovered too late.

You ordered this ode of the things that I love,
It's motion, music, and all ordered things,
Even though I question the joy that it brings.

I order my life and plan out my day,
(you say) What a waste of time, go find a mate.
I date all the time and I keep it in mind,
It's never too early to plan my escape.

Love is a drug, Huey Lewis said so,
But I don't do drugs, just masturbate.

You ordered this ode, and I alluded to order,
Have you followed along?
It stayed together, not even a quarter!

You ordered this ode, I tried to make sense,
I planned out my poem to the slightest word tense.

Love is confusing, yet I fill up my cup,
But when it comes to loving order, I need a prenup.

Love or order, love or order, love or order?
Listen to me order.
Your order is up.

Sigillum Dei

                          Hesitation
                          Over think
                          Holding back
                            Isolation

                          Desperation
                          Over stretch
                          Holding on
                            Oblivion

                          Automation
                           Over work
                          Holding fast
                          Emaciation

                            Satiation
                            Over full
                          Holding in
                          Suffocation

                            Creation
                            Overlook
                          Holding out
                          Desolation

                          Plantation
                            Over see
                          Holding loose
                          Emancipation

                          Transformation
                            Over now
                          Holding down
            Confirmation

Pride on My Side

Tension is high,
Faith is low,
We can't say goodbye,
To all that we know.

Forces ask why,
We reply with a "no",
We don't want to lie,
Or let feelings show.

It's not that we're shy,
Or don't' want to grow,
But we don't want to die,
For new seeds to sow.

So black out the sky,
Stand up in rows,
Muffle your cries,
And put on the show.

Time seems to fly,
Look there it goes,
How long before I,
Evolve the shadow.

Artificial Sugar

A time of trial,
A time of healing.
The sweet revile,
Of sly double dealing.

We take to kneeling,
We look for both.
A pleasant dealing,
Just not verbose.

Rejection hurts,
Despite your state.
Our shadows will skirt,
Not captivate.

We spend time to vet.
We spend time to parse.
With limits we correct,
Our boundaries from farse.

An actor knows,
The taste of lies.
Performs a dance,
With sideways eyes.

And so it goes,
Nothing but cinnamon.
Mixed in and drowned,
With thick icing on.

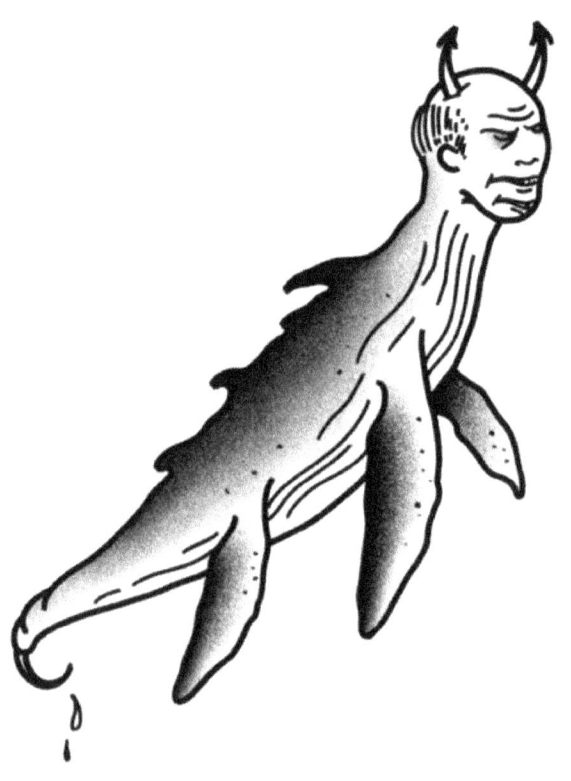

Acrobat of The Abyss

At a long empty table, with tall empty chairs,
I feel the sharp unstable, vessels tighten and snare.
Wind through broken windows, unexpectedly blunt,
Splinters of glass marking natures affront.

Pacing in circles, a line in stop-motion,
Deny, distract, imbibe; engage a reckless notion.
Follow back to inquire, find a theme to conspire,
Put ice on the pyre like a hitman for hire.

Lay out my entrails of internal combustion,
Reach up to the stars in fits of devotion.
The wind knocks me round, a white flash of reason,
I never do me proud; actions born of treason.

Exhale bitter tears, broken bricks against an ocean,
Stand up prostrate, all will against emotion.
The sun begins to set; I'm tired of myself,
Tangled and beset, and hazardous to health.

Innocent Talk

They will amuse, confuse, and become multi-use,
They are tools of the muse so frequently used.

They will define, confine, and draw all the lines,
They carry the power and possess the divine.

They will sell, tell, and be used to wish well,
They are the breakthrough shells and the body of spells.

They are healing, calming, and ruin good singing,
These symbols of logos hold all the true meaning.

Self - Awarewolf

Hidden influence:
Expel, repel, dispel!

Forgive me my trust,
My self-centered lust.
I can't help it, magnetic,
It's deathly genetic.

I lied on purpose,
I hid in plain sight.
A flirtatious mirage,
Given in to fleshed barrage.

Experiment with rest,
Experience enmeshed,
Edged up to the crest,
I know, I know me best.

Delicious Delight

What do I see waiting for me?
A symbol? An art?
A path to connect, all of the parts?

What do I hear creeping more near?
A hunter? Some prey?
Discovery of, alternative ways?

What do I know that time brings in tow?
A change? The same?
All that we can't, seem to attain?

What do I feel becoming more real?
A tribe? The I?
A shifting of our, dark paradigm?

What's that coming, faster than light?
All signs are sealed, well within sight.

We heard the winds, howling with fright,
The moment we steeled and decided to fight.
We knew that God would lend us his might,
And we felt the tides turn with delicious delight.

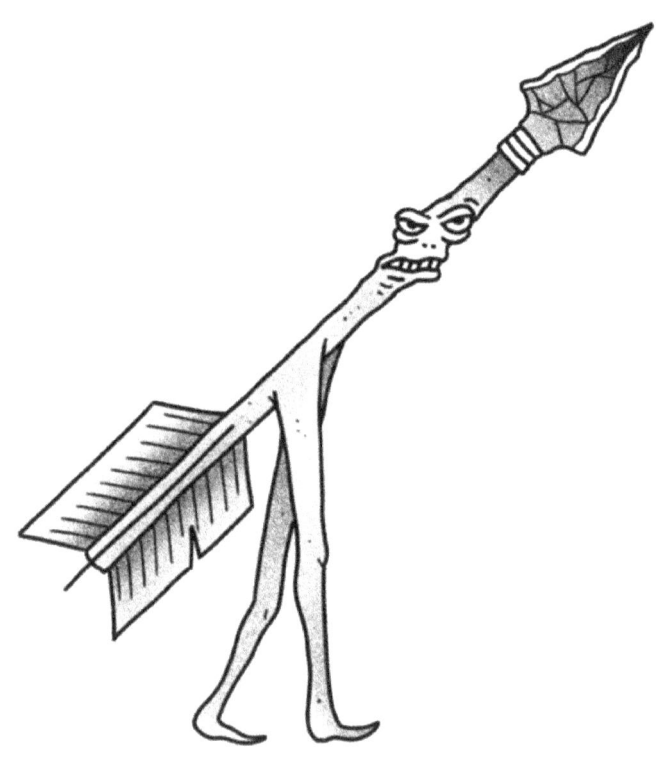

Obstinate Empathy

I gave in to the merge out of pure curiosity,
I was naive to the depths of shadow ferocity.

I found what you wanted kept silent,
Steeped in the words you worked from behind it.

I read all the tells, even childish cave scratches,
Of lying like whales in coded dispatches.

Twisted all omens, cried "inauspicious",
I did all I could to not be suspicious.

I found an affection deep in your tunnels,
A passion of self so violently bundled.

We all have the black, pushed deep in the back,
We only see it when it slips through the cracks.

My memories gaslit!
Trusting on faith just to move past it.

I beat with your heart and mirror your soul,
I dream on forever of swallowing you whole.

I found parts of me beneath the deliverance,
All four sides begging for severance.

Murky vibrations, loud yet reliant.
I struggle to listen and not be compliant.

Life Without a Pimp

      I got up early to catch my ship,
    The air was dry and cracked my lips.
   I poured some water and took a sip,
   Then knocked it over and had a slip.

I lay there spinning with my mind eclipsed,
     And as it happened, I broke my hip.
    I tried to stand but then went limp,
   There would not be another attempt.

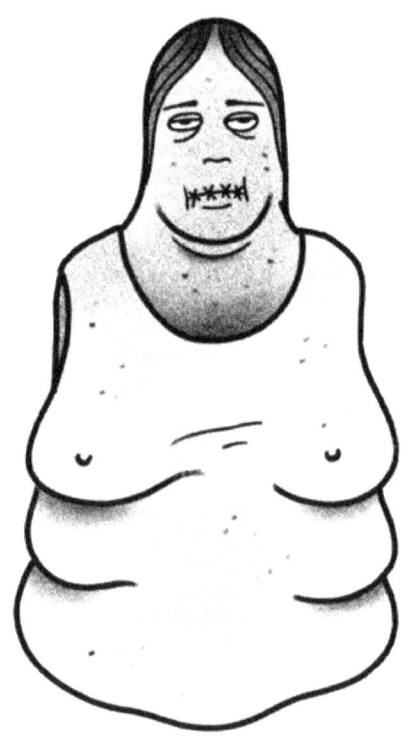

Chimerical Animus

Mirrored pain,
Every time.
The same refrain,
A lack of "mine."

Project the feeling,
The crowd will know.
You're not concealing,
You love the show.

A planted need.
Deep in your dirt.
A cheeky deed,
So long as it hurts.

"Just plant your seed!"
You cry out loud.
"I want to be freed,
Just do me proud."

Vibrations ring steep,
Anger without roots.
All touches you keep,
But the memory stands moot.

Postponed Percival

Show me respect,
The kind I deserve,
Naïve inner child,
You threw off the curve.

Affection in pounds,
Innocence abounds,
It's not my fault,
I exist by default.

Teasing the fuse,
Drinking my muse,
Sway forward to fast,
Gravity's contrast.

Keep checking the mail,
Tracks through the grass,
Delivery uncertain,
All sealed in the past.

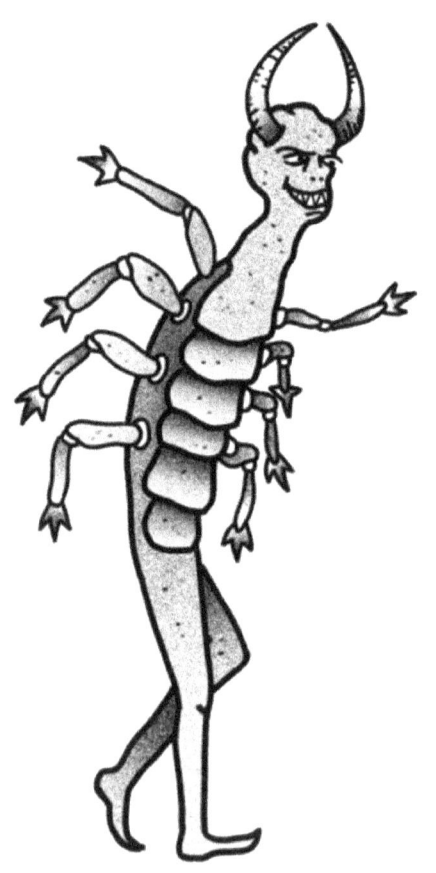

Elder Berries of The Salted Earth

Circumstances fall into angles for want of a straight line,
Down in thorned foliage and drowned in the brine,
Vixen hearts cry out for the pleasures of crime.

The world falls silent, flexed muscles or bust,
Betray all your beauty and withhold all your trust,
Mistaking faint echoes for tightly packed lust.

Puzzled ink hammers set out to conquer,
Curiosity sings static with no taste for honor,
Exiling wise notes for a trivial offer.

Secretly plan cities without any blight,
These hermits of shame, guilt, and hindsight,
Punish the man who hides in plain sight.

Ephemiracle

The pendulum reached out, turning its page,
Always in motion, usually off stage.
The players play along, no matter how strange,
It stays just the same, a constant exchange.

The water lays long, acting all natural,
Full of clear presence, touching it all.
Breaking down doors to fill up the halls,
It requests strong barrels to manage its fall.

The mountains stand stoic, digging in deep,
Further and further their tunnels will creep.
Hard to the core, with whoever they meet,
It needs loving whores, light on their feet.

The air talks softly, calling collect,
Often electric is how we detect it.
Its voice will be heard and highly respected,
It delights in the rush to arrive unexpected.

The flames jump up, giving no care,
Moving in fast and laying out bare,
The soul on display, striving to share,
It settles at random; always beware.

The pendulum leaned in, showing its rage,
Uniquely in frame and absent of age.
The momentum builds and never is caged,
It works without effort, always engaged.

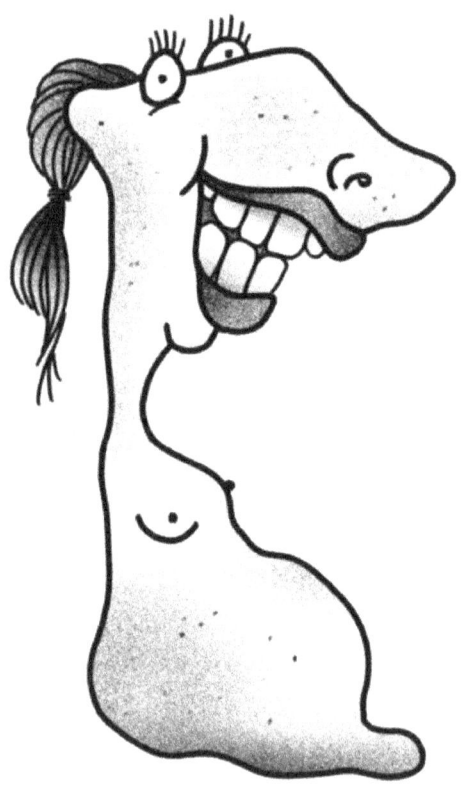

Median Patience

Stand and wait,
Seeking your mate,
Risk if you dare,
Accepting your fate.

Rewards can be great,
By changing your state,
Yet always beware,
To walk the line straight.

Moving to slow,
You stay quite alone,
Growing to hate,
To weakness you're prone.

But acting in haste,
Life you will waste,
So do plan with care,
And love you will taste.

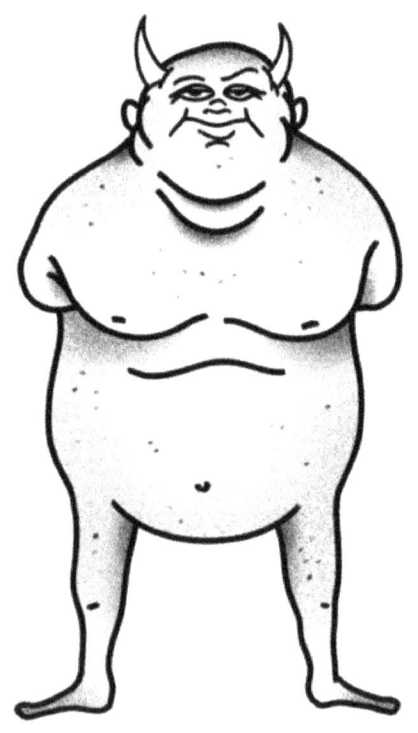

To Commune

I float on the waves of shared memory,
Surfing the flow and connecting to tense,
Gravity pulls and I have no defense.

Engulfed in the tow as my ears pop to silence,
Panic made wet, I choke in the mist,
Yellow flags are displayed, and I can't resist.

Held out by the tide, and just out of reach,
A spiritual Pax,
A movement in speech.

To answer all prayers,
To hyper-transcend,
I wake with eyes closed, not fully aware.

I will the vibration,
But Heaven can wait!
I think and I think.

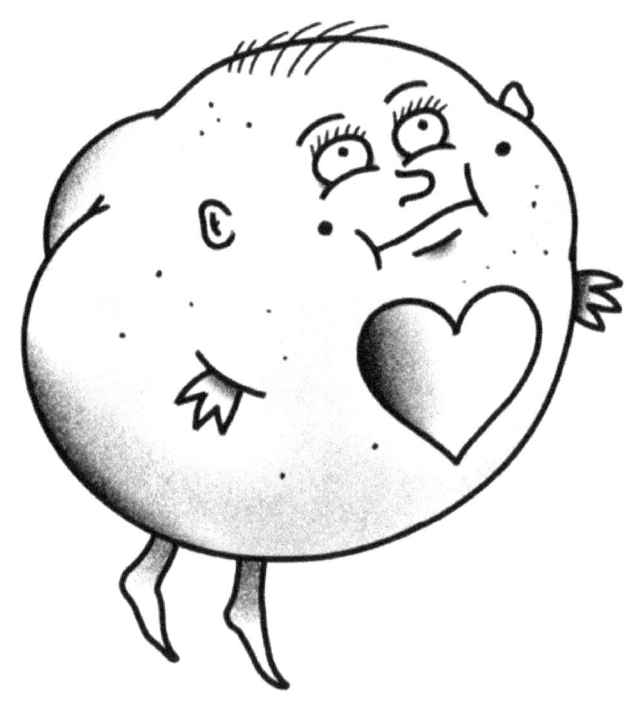

Devour Maternal

I float above ground,
I feel but don't touch,
My feet do not drag,
I'm puffed up too much.

I'm three sizes too big,
I'm less heavy than full,
I take up no space,
But I make all the rules.

I dance to this game,
I'm far from ashamed,
I indulge without care,
And I never play fair.

I see what I want,
I'm close but too far,
I reach but don't clutch,
I don't care who you are.

The risk I will take,
It must be this way,
Your heart I will take,
Or mine will decay.

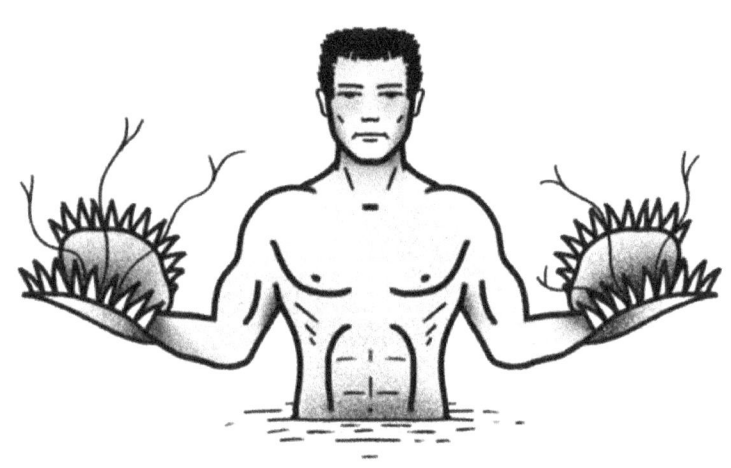

Level Up

I opened your box with tears in my eyes,
The emotions packed neatly and folded to size.
I imagined you silent, packing so fine,
This is the last time you touched things of mine.

Holding on tightly, a last shred of hope,
Your heart begged for release before it was closed.
That feeling of finality under layers of tape,
A volatile artifact tied tight at the nape.

You opened my heart with stars in your eyes,
The emotions buried deep but spilling the sides.
You imagined me pure with wisdom unfound,
The moment it opened we unbuckled our bounds.

Holding on tightly with no hint of escape,
My heart was sacrificial; could I have known?
That feeling of finality under layers of tape,
A cheap cardboard nest, no longer at home.

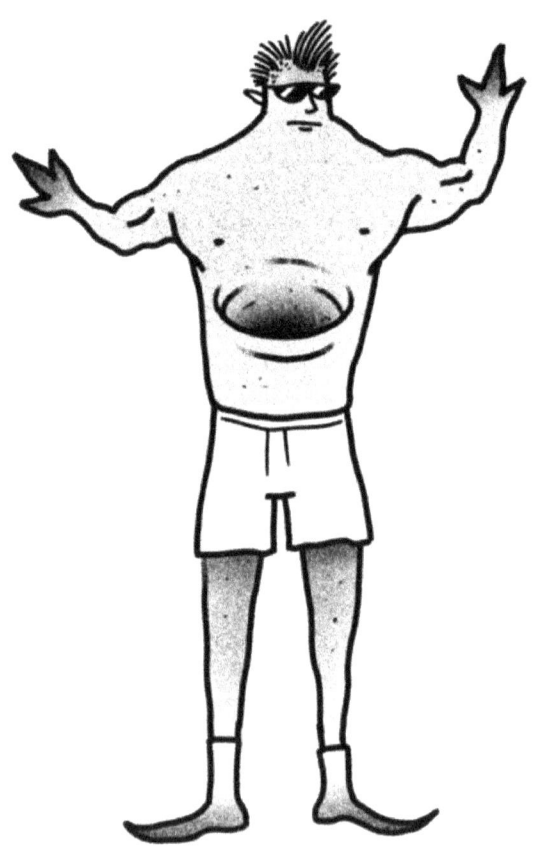

Macho Robusto

Cracked leather in a smoke-filled room,
Hints of past action with an aura that looms,
Thinking without thoughts of impending doom.

Low heart rates in final male bastions,
Loving aesthetics with no hint of passion,
Seems everything suffers, after a fashion.

All of my digits full of broken cell flirts,
Inhale once again seeking more alerts,
Another sip of wine to make me more inert.

I made all my mistakes with vanity up front,
Dropped back hard but still couldn't punt,
Pointed all my rakes in a joyous pride hunt.

Exhale dirty air with lead on silver feet,
Pay the butcher double for the wrong cut of meat.
A muscle car throwing rods down a one-way street.

Fear Filled Fealty

A touch of silence,
The pain of open space.
Societal defiance,
I'm Just saving face.

Too cool for school,
Too desperate for meaning.
Just playing the fool,
That's what I'm screaming.

God-made paths cave,
Past the thermocline.
Deep beneath the waves,
Away from fishing lines.

Find the rocks of reason,
The nuance small as sand.
Don't stop believing,
A journey through my hands.

Skin screams in brail,
Lightly making steam.
Pipes of faith turn pale,
Never wanting to be seen.

Push Pull

Mid-week brunch, or sea level high-rise,
Classic to the eyes, but shift with the tides.
Universal difference, with relative instance,
Not yet ready, to go the full distance.

Clearly visible, or all cloaked in throws,
Open to muse, but without a way through.
Universal shape, with relative approach,
Not in the position, to shrug off reproach.

Moving too fast, or missing the bus,
Built to maintain, but curves urging flight.
Universal labor, with relative favor,
Try as I might, there's no resisting the flavor.

Passionate thinking, or reasoned emotion,
Show up on time, but never to dine.
Universal motions, with relative devotion,
No longer dumb enough for all this commotion.

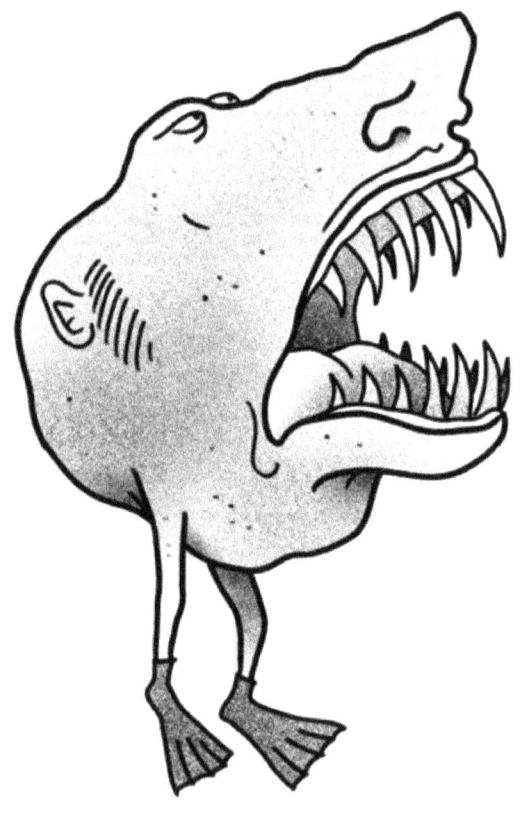

Playbook

Sell nostalgia to those in the past,
And holiday foods a year in advance.

Concoct ideals for those far ahead,
Just out of reach with a slight hint of dread.

Pleasure upon pleasure for those in the now,
Stimulated skin & milked dry sacred cows.

Sell all the goods to those who are bad,
Petty pretty wares in bulk my good lad.

Concoct hungry health for those who seek glory,
Bogged down in tech, no original stories.

Pleasure upon pleasure for those of steep measure,
Long legs, big dicks, and a fat bank ledger.

Sell out tradition to those who have none,
Boil popped nihilists who think we're all one.

Concoct a tall tale for those who would bite,
Get fat on hot air and lose all their fight.

Pleasure upon pleasure for those who would kneel,
Dash all their hopes, the art of the deal.

Acknowledgements: Bianca Clark, John Denmat, Al, Jeff, and Earl at the cigar lounge, and all the baristas at my local coffee shop: thank you for all the support, encouragement, criticisms, and conversation.

J. Friedrich Allyn is a native of the American South. He enjoys furniture that identifies as contemporary industrial art nuevo flirting with mid-century modern art deco, medieval religious symbolism in the background of photographs, hurtful snap judgements over petty character traits, temperature control, the mechanics of context, the many moods of language, personal atmosphere stylization, the liminal arts, being secure with insecurities, reckless words, cringe puns, courageous observation, home grown fruit, store bought wine, paradoxical aphoristic axioms, archival simplicity, occult based political analysis, causal arguments with an esoteric premise, stone-faced gaslighting in the face of emotional authoritarianism, responding to subjective preferences with meta-objectivity, werewolves in vampire clothing, and snooty seltzer water.

www.ingramcontent.com/pod-product-compliance
Lightning Source LLC
Chambersburg PA
CBHW032144040426
42449CB00005B/396